Movement Poems

Compiled by John Foster

Contents

Acknowledgements

The Editor and Publisher wish to thank the following who have kindly given permission for the use of copyright material:

Marie Brookes for 'Move along, please' © 1995 Marie Brookes; Angi Holden for 'Our dishwasher' © 1995 Angi Holden; Julie Holder for 'Jelly wobble' and 'First steps' both © 1995 Julie Holder; Richard James for 'My machine' © 1995 Richard James; Daphne Lister for 'Playthings' © 1995 Daphne Lister; Marian Swinger for 'Bouncing to the moon' © 1995 Marian Swinger.

Move along, please

Sally skips
Hamid hops
Charlie crawls
Frankie flops.

Rupinder rolls
Cathy creeps
Sameena strolls
Laura leaps.

Dilip dances
William wobbles
Jimmy jogs
Hannah hobbles.

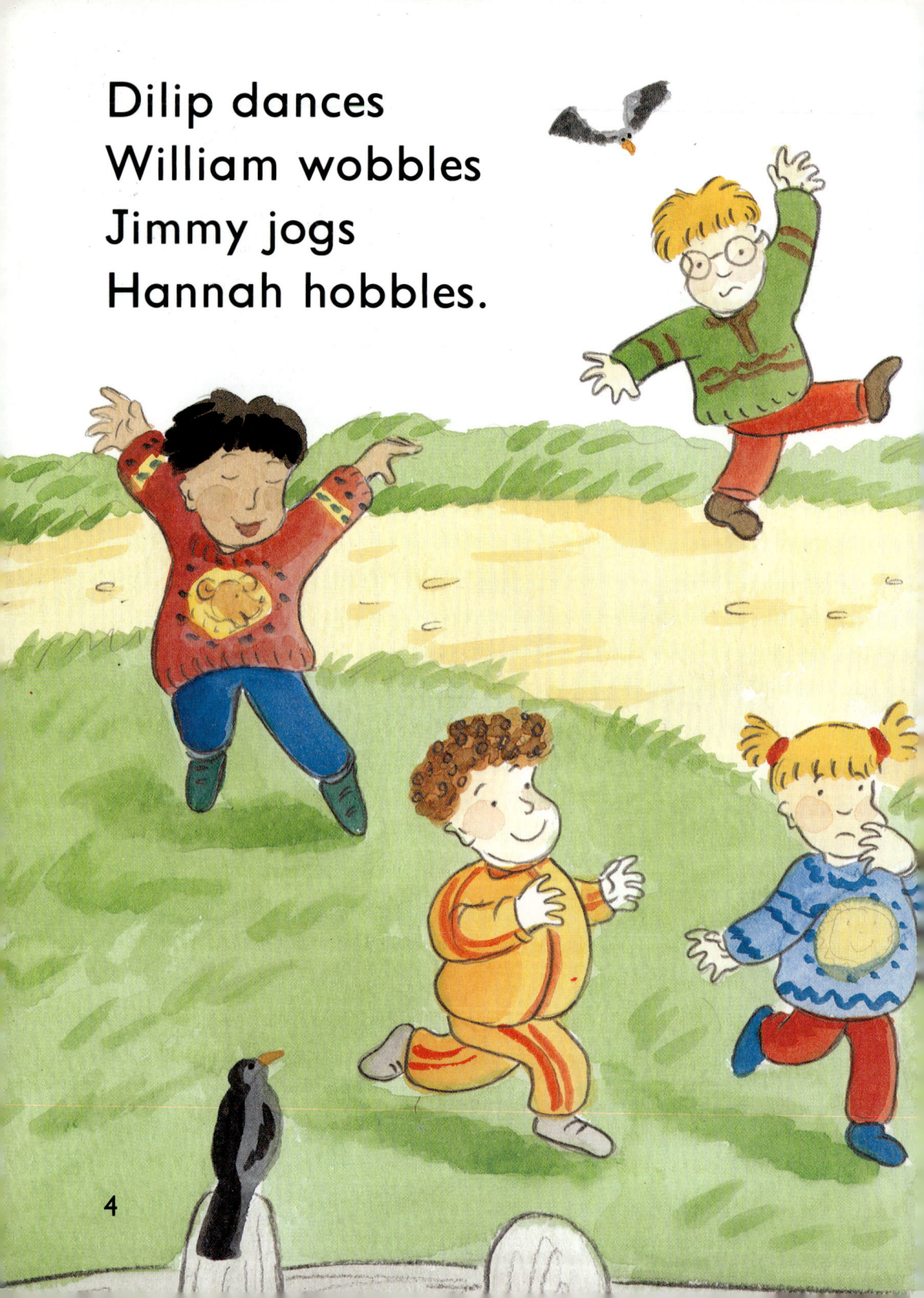

Jack jumps
Steven stalks
Richard runs
and I walk!

Marie Brookes

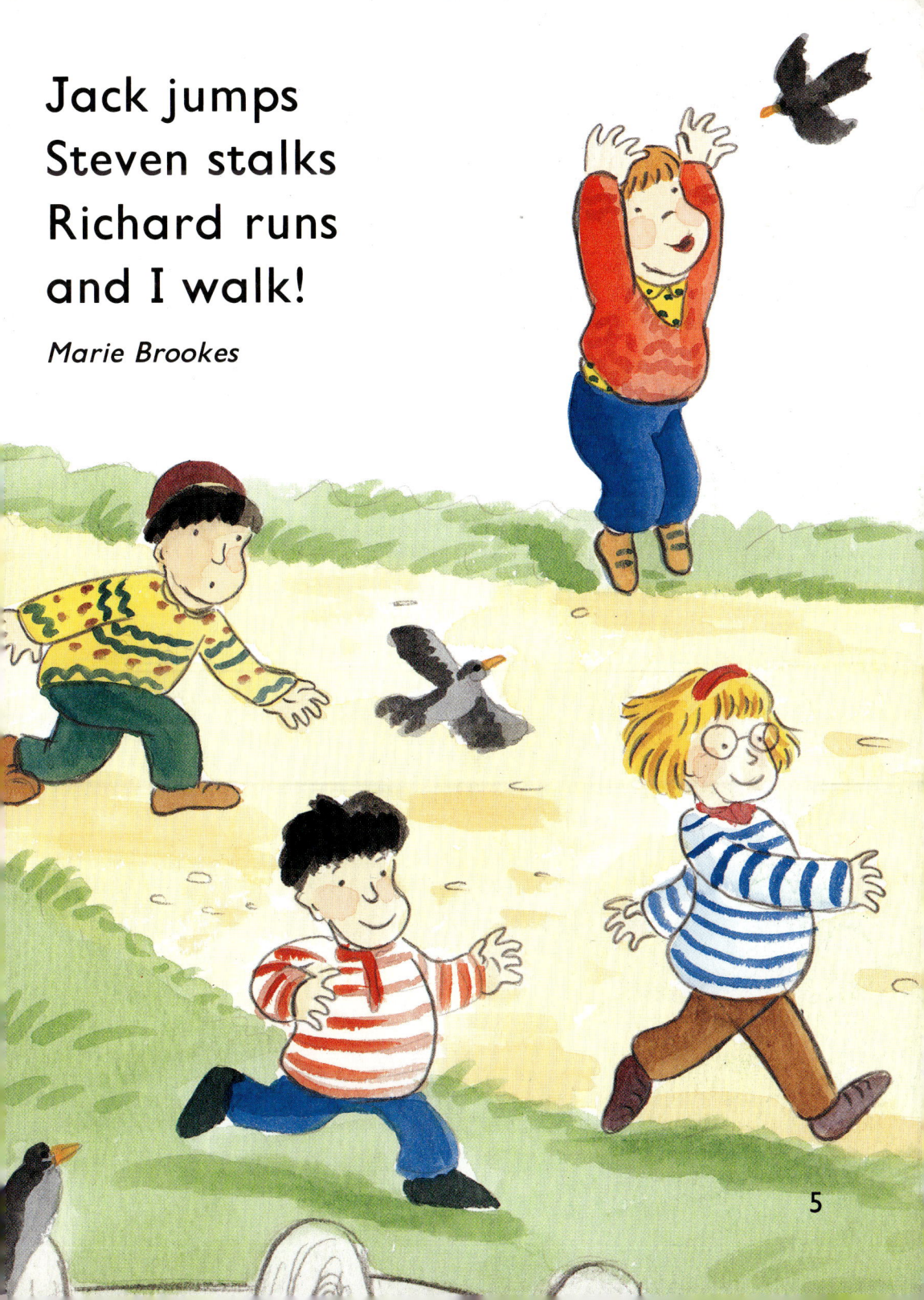

Jelly wobble

A butterfly can flutter.
A worm can squirm.
A snake can wriggle
On its belly.

A fish can flop.
Water can slop.
But nothing
Can wobble
Like a jelly.

Julie Holder

First steps

One step, two steps,
The baby toddles.
Three steps, four steps,
The baby wobbles.
Five steps, six steps,
The baby falls flat.
My mum says I used to do that.

Julie Holder

My machine

It's got knobs you can twiddle,
And bells you can ring,
It's got bits you can waggle,
And things you can ping.

It's got levers you pull,
It's got wheels that whizz round,
And what does it make?
Just a wonderful sound!

Richard James

Our dishwasher

Our dishwasher splishes
and sploshes and mumbles.
It grunts and it groans.
It gurgles and grumbles.

There's suds on the floor.
It bubbles like mad.
But it's not a machine,
it's only my dad!

Angi Holden

Playthings

Can you bounce, bounce, bounce
like a big, bouncy ball,
trying to look over
the garden wall?

Can you float, float, float
like a bright balloon,
sailing through the air
on its way to the moon?

Daphne Lister

Bouncing to the moon

We're on a bouncy castle.
We'll be jumping off it soon,
unless you pull the plug out
and we whizz off to the moon.

Marian Swinger